THE FABULOUS LOST & FOUND

AND THE LITTLE MOUSE WHO SPOKE TAGALOG

WRITTEN BY MARK PALLIS
ILLUSTRATED BY PETER BAYNTON

NEU WESTEND
— PRESS —

Thanks Amae Dechavez-Barcia - MP

For Hannah and Skye - PB

THE FABULOUS LOST & FOUND AND THE LITTLE MOUSE WHO SPOKE TAGALOG
Copyright text © 2020 Mark Pallis and Copyright images © 2020 Peter Baynton

All rights reserved. This book or any portion thereof may not be reproduced or used in any manner whatsoever without the express written permission of the publisher except for the use of brief excerpts in a review.

First Printing, 2020
ISBN 978-1-9160801-8-8
NeuWestendPress.com

THE FABULOUS LOST & FOUND

AND THE LITTLE MOUSE WHO SPOKE TAGALOG

WRITTEN BY MARK PALLIS
ILLUSTRATED BY PETER BAYNTON

NEU WESTEND
— PRESS —

In the middle of the big city is a tiny yellow building. If anyone loses anything, this is where it ends up.

It is called the Lost and Found.

Mr and Mrs Frog keep everything safe, hoping that someday every lost watch and bag and phone and toy and shoe and cheesegrater will find its owner again.

But the shop is very small. And there are so many lost things. It is all quite a squeeze, but still, it's fabulous.

One sunny day, a little mouse walked in.

"Welcome," said Mrs Frog. "What have you lost?"

"Naiwala ko ang aking sumbrero," said the mouse.

Mr and Mrs Frog could not speak Tagalog. They had no idea what the little mouse was saying.

What shall we do? they wondered.

Maybe she's lost an umbrella. Everyone loses an umbrella at least twice, thought Mr Frog.

"Have you lost this?" asked Mr Frog.

"Isang payong? Hindi," replied the mouse.

Then Mrs Frog remembered something that had been handed in a few months ago…

"Is this yours?" Mrs Frog asked, holding up a chunk of cheese.

"Keso? Hindi. Mabaho!" said the mouse.

"Time to put that cheese in the bin dear," said Mr Frog.

"Maybe the word 'sumbrero' means coat," said Mr Frog.

"Now where did I put that nice yellow one?"

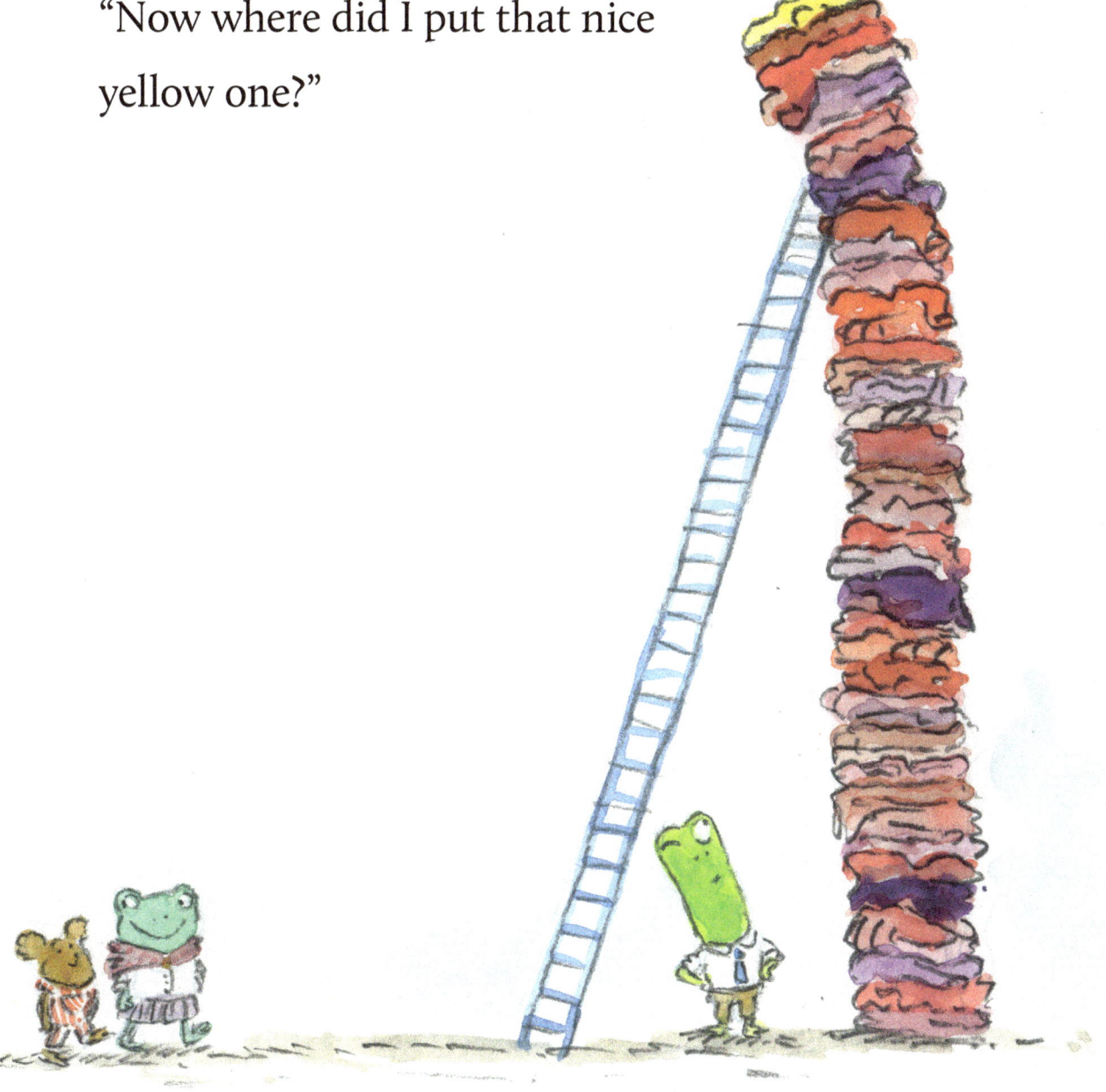

"Got it!" said Mr Frog.

"Pang-ginaw? Hindi. Naiwala ko ang aking sumbrero," said the mouse.

She was starting to feel a bit frustrated.

"We need to keep trying," said Mrs Frog.

Hindi scarf.

Hindi pantalon.

Hindi suweter.

Hindi sapatos.

Hindi shades.

"Naiwala ko ang aking sumbrero," said the mouse.

Hindi tatlong libro.

Hindi apat na saging.

Hindi limang susi.

It was no good. A fat wet tear rolled down the mouse's cheek.

"How about a nice cup of tea?" asked Mrs Frog kindly.

"Gustong gusto ko ng tsaa. Salamat," replied the mouse.
They sat together, sipping their tea and all feeling a bit sad.

Suddenly, the mouse realised she could try pointing.

She pointed at her head.
"Sumbrero!" she said.

"I've got it!" exclaimed Mrs Frog, leaping up.

"A wig of course!" said Mrs Frog.

"Hindi peluka," said the mouse.

Hindi pula.

Hindi malaginto.

Hindi kayumanggi.

Hindi iba't-ibang kulay.

Hindi berde.

"What about this?" asked Mr Frog, pulling back a curtain.

"Sumbrero!" exclaimed the mouse.

"Ah, so 'sumbrero' means hat. Wonderful!" Mr and Mrs Frog cheered.

Masyadong mataas.

Masyadong maliit.

Masyadong malaki.

Masyadong masikip.

"One hat left," said Mrs Frog, reaching all the way to the back of the cupboard.

"It couldn't be this old thing, could it?"

"Ang aking sumbrero.

Nakita ko na ang aking sumbrero!

Maraming salamat," said the mouse.

And just like that, the mouse found her hat.

"Paalam," she said, as she skipped away.
"Paalam," replied Mr and Mrs Frog.

"I wonder who will come tomorrow?" said Mr Frog.
Mrs Frog put her arm around him.

"I don't know," she replied, giving him a squeeze,
"but whoever it is, we'll do our best to help."

LEARNING TO LOVE LANGUAGES

An additional language opens a child's mind, broadens their horizons and enriches their emotional life. Research has shown that the time between a child's birth and their sixth or seventh birthday is a "golden period" when they are most receptive to new languages. This is because they have an in-built ability to distinguish the sounds they hear and make sense of them. The Story-powered Language Learning Method taps into these natural abilities.

HOW THE STORY-POWERED LANGUAGE LEARNING METHOD WORKS

We create an emotionally engaging and funny story for children and adults to enjoy together, just like any other picture book. Studies show that social interaction, like enjoying a book together, is critical in language learning.

Through the story, we introduce a relatable character who speaks only in the new language. This helps build empathy and a positive attitude towards people who speak different languages. These are both important aspects in laying the foundations for lasting language acquisition in a child's life.

As the story progresses, the child naturally works with the characters to discover the meaning of a wide range of fun new words. Strategic use of humour ensures that this subconscious learning is rewarded with laughter; the child feels good and the first seeds of a lifelong love of languages are sown.

For more information and free downloads visit www.neuwestendpress.com

ALL THE BEAUTIFUL TAGALOG WORDS AND PHRASES FROM OUR STORY

Tagalog	English
Naiwala ko ang aking sumbrero	I've lost my hat
payong	umbrella
keso	cheese
mabaho	it stinks
pang-ginaw	coat
scarf	scarf
pantalon	trousers
shades	sunglasses
suweter	sweater
sapatos	shoes
isa	one
dalawa	two
tatlo	three
apat	four
lima	five
kompyuter	computer
libro	book
susi	key
saging	banana
bisikleta	bicycle
gustong gusto ko ng tsaa	I love tea
salamat	thank you
peluka	wig
pula	red
malaginto	blond
kayumanggi	brown
berde	green
iba't ibang kulay	multicoloured
hindi	no
ang aking sumbrero	my hat
masyadong mataas	too tall (object e.g hat)
masyadong malaki	too big
masyadong maliit	too small
masyadong masikip	too tight
nakita ko na ang aking sumbrero	I've found my hat
maraming salamat	thank you very much
paalam	goodbye

THE WORLD OF
THE FABULOUS LOST & FOUND

THIS STORY IS ALSO AVAILABLE IN...

FRENCH SPANISH
ITALIAN CZECH
KOREAN WELSH
GERMAN HEBREW
SWEDISH POLISH SLOVAKIAN
VIETNAMESE LATIN PORTUGUESE

...AND MANY MORE LANGUAGES!

@MARK_PALLIS ON TWITTER
WWW.MARKPALLIS.COM

ENJOYED IT?
WRITE A REVIEW AND
LET US KNOW!

@PETERBAYNTON ON INSTAGRAM
WWW.PETERBAYNTON.COM

www.ingramcontent.com/pod-product-compliance
Lightning Source LLC
Chambersburg PA
CBHW042030100526
44587CB00029B/4358